THE KINGSTONE BIBLE
VOLUME ONE

KINGSTONE
COMICS

THE KINGSTONE BIBLE
V O L U M E   O N E

Published by Kingstone Comics
www.KingstoneComics.com
Copyright © 2011
Printed in the USA

KINGSTONE
COMICS

CONTENTS

IN THE BEGINNING, BEFORE THE FIRST MAN WAS CREATED, BEFORE THE EARTH, THE SUN, THE STARS, EVEN BEFORE LIGHT AND TIME WERE CREATED, THERE WAS *GOD*.

HE ALONE EXISTED WITHOUT BEGINNING, BUT HE WAS NOT LONELY. UNLIKE FINITE MAN, GOD EXISTS SIMULTANEOUSLY AS THREE PERSONS IN ONE. EACH DISTINCT PERSON IS CO-EQUAL AND CO-ETERNAL, ONE IN ESSENCE, NATURE, POWER, ACTION, AND WILL. HE COMMUNED WITH HIMSELF IN HARMONIOUS LOVE.

BUT GOD WANTED TO SHARE HIS LIFE. HE WANTED FRIENDS AND NEIGHBORS.

THE BIBLE* TELLS US GOD CREATED NUMEROUS KINDS OF ANGELIC BEINGS TO OFFER PRAISE AROUND HIS THRONE, BUT ONE CALLED LUCIFER LED A THIRD OF THEM IN REBELLION. GOD CAST THEM OUT OF HEAVEN AND LUCIFER'S NAME WAS CHANGED TO SATAN.

BUT THIS IS NOT THEIR STORY.

THIS IS THE STORY OF GOD WORKING WITH MANKIND.

*SEE PAGE 321 FOR A BRIEF DESCRIPTION OF THE BOOK CALLED THE BIBLE. FOR MORE INFORMATION ABOUT SATAN SEE: ISAIAH 14:12-14, 45:18; EZEKIEL 28:13-19; MATTHEW 25:41; LUKE 10:18; REVELATION 12:4, 20:2

IN THE BEGINNING GOD CREATED
THE HEAVEN AND THE EARTH.
AND IT CAME TO PASS THAT
THE EARTH WAS FORMLESS AND
VOID, AND THE CREATOR MOVED
UPON THE FACE OF THE WATERS.

SUDDENLY GOD SPOKE
INTO THE DARKNESS...

"LET THERE BE LIGHT"

IT WAS NOT AS MANY MODERN MEN
SUPPOSE. THE CREATOR DID NOT MAKE USE
OF EVOLUTION. HE CREATED ALL THINGS BY
SIMPLY SPEAKING THEM INTO EXISTENCE.
IN SIX DAYS GOD MADE PLANTS AND
ANIMALS TO POPULATE THE EARTH.

HISSSSS...

THE SERPENT DECEIVED ME. HE TOLD ME I WOULDN'T DIE, THAT I WOULD BE LIKE YOU, BUT I AM NOT LIKE YOU. I FEEL AWFUL.

SO GOD CURSED THE SERPENT AND SAID UNTO HIM...

BECAUSE YOU HAVE DONE THIS, I WILL MAKE YOU CRAWL ON YOUR BELLY AND GET DUST IN YOUR MOUTH.

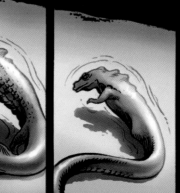

I WILL MAKE YOUR SEED AND THE WOMAN'S CHILD TO BE ENEMIES. YOUR SEED WILL BRUISE THE HEEL OF THE WOMAN'S CHILD, BUT HE WILL BRUISE YOUR HEAD.

HERE IS PROMISE OF A FUTURE BATTLE. A TIME WILL COME WHEN THE WOMAN'S SEED WILL DEFEAT SATAN. THIS PERSON WILL REDEEM MANKIND BACK TO GOD AND DELIVER THEM FROM THE CURSE OF SIN AND DEATH.

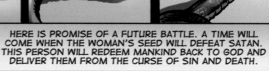

GOD COULD HAVE DESTROYED LUCIFER AND ALL HIS ANGELS IN JUST A MOMENT'S TIME, BUT HE ALLOWED THEM TO LIVE AS A TEST FOR THE HUMAN RACE. WILL MEN FOLLOW GOD, OR WILL THEY FOLLOW SATAN IN HIS REBELLION?

ADAM AND EVE HAD MANY CHILDREN. LATER, THEIR SONS AND DAUGHTERS WOULD MARRY EACH OTHER AND HAVE CHILDREN OF THEIR OWN.

THEIR FIRST SON, CAIN, GREW VEGETABLES AND FRUIT. THEIR SECOND SON, ABEL, RAISED ANIMALS. COULD IT BE THAT ONE OF THEM WOULD BE THE PROMISED SON WHO WOULD DESTROY SATAN?

CAIN AND ABEL KNEW ABOUT GOD AND THE EVENTS IN THE GARDEN. BUT GOD NO LONGER WALKED AND TALKED WITH HUMANITY. ADAM AND ALL HIS DESCENDENTS WERE SEPARATED FROM GOD BY ADAM'S DISOBEDIENCE. LIFE WAS HARD WITHOUT GOD.

THERE CAME A DAY WHEN THE TWO SONS DECIDED TO WORSHIP GOD. THEIR FATHER HAD TOLD THEM OF GOD KILLING THE ANIMALS IN THE GARDEN, SO BY FAITH ABLE SLEW AN ANIMAL AND OFFERED IT TO GOD.

OH, GOD, I AM A SINFUL MAN; I KILL THIS LAMB AND OFFER IT TO YOU IN THE PLACE OF MY OWN DEATH.

CAIN MADE AN OFFERING OF THE BEST HE HAD, BUT IT WAS NOT A BLOOD SACRIFICE. CAIN DID NOT UNDERSTAND THAT HIS SIN OFFENDED GOD.

GOD, PLEASE ACCEPT THIS GIFT OF THE BEST I HAVE TO OFFER.

WILL ONE OF THESE MEN BE THE PROMISED REDEEMER?

NO, CAIN

GOD WAS PLEASED WITH ABEL AND HIS OFFERING. WHEN HE SAW THE SHEDDING OF THE BLOOD OF THE INNOCENT LAMB, GOD PUT AWAY ABEL'S SIN.

GOD SAID TO CAIN, "IF YOU DO WHAT YOU SHOULD I WILL BE PLEASED WITH YOU. ALSO, YOU WILL RULE OVER YOUR BROTHER ABEL, AND HE WILL LIVE IN SUBJECTION TO YOU."

GOD REJECTED CAIN'S OFFERING BECAUSE IT WAS WITHOUT BLOOD.

WHO DO YOU THINK YOU ARE? MY FRUIT AND VEGETABLES ARE WORTH MORE THAN THAT BLOODY LAMB. WHAT MAKES YOU SO SPECIAL?

MY BROTHER, THERE IS STILL TIME TO OFFER A BLOOD SACRIFICE.

I'VE HAD ALL OF THIS I'M GOING TO TAKE!

WHACK!

ABEL DIED, AND CAIN TRIED TO HIDE HIS SIN OF MURDER.

SETH HAD A SON, AND HIS SON HAD A SON, AND MANY MORE SONS WERE BORN, BUT STILL NONE CAME FORTH TO REMOVE THE CURSE OF SIN AND DESTROY DEATH. SOON THE EARTH WAS POPULATED WITH MANY CITIES, VILLAGES, AND FARMS.

WITH EACH NEW GENERATION, AS THE PEOPLE INCREASED, SIN INCREASED. THE PEOPLE COMMITTED SEXUAL SINS AND WERE VIOLENT. EVERY THOUGHT WAS SINFUL. NO ONE LIVED RIGHTEOUSLY. ADAM HAD COMMITTED ONE SIN; THE PEOPLE NOW COMMITTED MANY SINS.

GOD SAID, "I REGRET I MADE MAN ON THE EARTH. I WILL DESTROY EVERY THING THAT IS ALIVE ON THE EARTH." SATAN, WHO HATES GOD'S KINGDOM, WOULD BE PLEASED TO SEE GOD KILL EVERYONE.

NINE GENERATIONS HAD NOW PASSED (1,400 YEARS) AND THE WORLD WAS FILLED WITH SIN.

MEN MADE SLAVES OF THEIR FELLOW MAN.

WILL GOD EVER HAVE A FAMILY TO LOVE HIM AND WALK IN OBEDIENCE?

THERE'S NOT MUCH ROOM LEFT.

THIS IS THE LAST OF THEM.

NOAH, IT IS TIME, COME INTO THE BOAT WITH ALL YOUR FAMILY AND THE ANIMALS. IT WILL SOON BE TOO LATE FOR ALL THOSE WHO REFUSED TO STOP SINNING.

GOD SHUT THE DOOR TO THE BOAT, AND FOR SEVEN DAYS NOTHING HAPPENED.

HA, HA, LOOK AT THE FOOLS, SHUT UP IN A BIG BOAT WITH ALL THOSE ANIMALS IN THE MIDDLE OF A DRY PLAIN, MILES FROM ANY WATER.

YEAH, I BET THE LIONS HAVE EATEN THEM BY NOW.

THEY HAVE BEEN IN THERE A WEEK!

BUT ON THE SEVENTH DAY IT BEGAN TO RAIN, AND WATER STORED DEEP IN THE EARTH CAME TO THE SURFACE.

I HAVE NEVER SEEN ANYTHING LIKE THIS; DO YOU THINK THE CRAZY PEOPLE IN THE BOAT COULD BE RIGHT ABOUT GOD WANTING TO KILL EVERYBODY FOR THEIR SINS?

DON'T BE RIDICULOUS; GOD IS LOVE. HOW COULD ONE MAN BE RIGHT AND ALL OUR RELIGIOUS LEADERS BE WRONG?

BEFORE THIS TIME, IT HAD NEVER RAINED. THE WEATHER WAS ALWAYS NICE AND A MIST CAME UP FROM THE EARTH TO WATER THE GROUND. NO ONE HAD EVER SEEN OR HEARD OF RAIN, SO MANY PEOPLE THOUGHT NOAH WAS CRAZY FOR THINKING WATER WAS GOING TO FALL FROM THE SKY, BUT NOAH BELIEVED WHAT GOD SAID.

I SHOULD HAVE LISTENED TO NOAH. WHAT A FOOL I HAVE BEEN!

GOD, SAVE MY BABY!

BEFORE LONG THE BOAT SETTLED ON A MOUNTAINTOP CALLED ARARAT. EVERYONE CAME OUT TO A NEW WORLD, A WORLD WITHOUT SIN.

NOAH BUILT AN ALTAR AND OFFERED ANIMAL SACRIFICES TO GOD. THOUGH NOAH WAS A JUST MAN, THERE WAS STILL SIN IN HIS HEART. THESE BLOOD SACRIFICES WERE OFFERED TO GOD IN SUBSTITUTION FOR THE LIVES OF NOAH AND ALL HIS FAMILY.

THE ANIMALS REPRESENTED THE EIGHT WHO SHOULD HAVE DIED IN THE FLOOD, BUT WERE SPARED BY THE GRACE OF GOD. IT WAS SOMETHING LIKE WHAT GOD DID IN THE GARDEN WHEN HE KILLED ANIMALS TO MAKE COVERINGS FOR ADAM AND EVE.

I WILL GIVE YOU A RAINBOW IN THE SKY AS A REMINDER THAT I WILL NEVER AGAIN DESTROY THE EARTH WITH WATER. YOU SHOULD HAVE MANY CHILDREN AND SCATTER OUT TO REPOPULATE THE WHOLE EARTH.

I WILL MAKE ANIMALS TO FEAR MEN. YOU MAY EAT ANY CREATURE THAT IS ALIVE AND CRAWLING ON THE EARTH, JUST AS YOU EAT VEGETABLES AND HERBS, BUT YOU ARE NOT TO EAT THE BLOOD OF ANY CREATURE. DO NOT KILL ANYONE.

IF SOMEONE IS FOUND TO BE GUILTY OF KILLING ANOTHER, THEN HE IS TO BE KILLED BY OTHER MEN. IF A MAN SHEDS THE BLOOD OF ANOTHER MAN, THEN OTHER MEN SHOULD SHED HIS BLOOD TO PAY FOR HIS CRIME, BECAUSE THE LIFE IS IN THE BLOOD.

NOAH BECAME A FARMER AND PLANTED GRAPES. THE NEW WORLD WAS LONELY WITH JUST FOUR FAMILIES, BUT SOON HIS SONS WERE HAVING CHILDREN OF THEIR OWN.

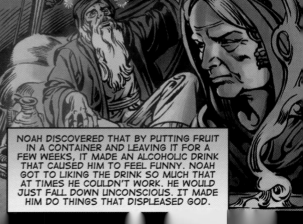

NOAH DISCOVERED THAT BY PUTTING FRUIT IN A CONTAINER AND LEAVING IT FOR A FEW WEEKS, IT MADE AN ALCOHOLIC DRINK THAT CAUSED HIM TO FEEL FUNNY. NOAH GOT TO LIKING THE DRINK SO MUCH THAT AT TIMES HE COULDN'T WORK. HE WOULD JUST FALL DOWN UNCONSCIOUS. IT MADE HIM DO THINGS THAT DISPLEASED GOD.

APPROXIMATELY 2247 B.C.

NOAH'S SON, HAM, HAD A SON NAMED CUSH, AND THEN CUSH HAD A SON NAMED NIMROD. NIMROD GREW UP TO BE A MIGHTY HUNTER, AND WAS WELL KNOWN THROUGHOUT THE WHOLE EARTH. HE REFUSED TO OBEY GOD AND STARTED HIS OWN FALSE RELIGION IN A PLACE CALLED BABYLON.

THE PEOPLE OF BABYLON DID NOT WANT TO SCATTER OUT AND REPOPULATE THE EARTH AS GOD HAD COMMANDED, SO THEY GOT TOGETHER AND BUILT A GREAT AND HIGH TOWER AS A CENTER OF WORSHIP.

BUT IT WAS NOT THEIR CREATOR THEY WORSHIPED. SATAN LED THEM TO CREATE THEIR OWN GODS OUT OF WOOD, STONE, AND METAL.

GOD WAS ANGRY AT THEIR REFUSAL TO SCATTER OVER THE EARTH, SO HE CAUSED THE PEOPLE TO SPEAK MANY DIFFERENT LANGUAGES.

THE WORKMEN COULD NO LONGER UNDERSTAND EACH OTHER, SO THEY COULD NOT CONTINUE THE WORK.

EACH LANGUAGE GROUP WENT ITS OWN WAY. SOME PEOPLE WENT TO DISTANT PLACES IN THE EARTH, SOME TRAVELED IN SHIPS TO DISTANT ISLANDS, SOME TO THE NORTH WHERE IT WAS COLD AND SOME DOWN INTO THE DESERTS WHERE IT WAS HOT. SO GOD'S COMMAND TO REPOPULATE THE EARTH WAS FULFILLED.

AS THE EARTH WAS FILLED WITH PEOPLE, SIN AGAIN INCREASED. THE PEOPLE BOWED DOWN TO IDOLS AND FORGOT THE LIVING GOD.

Moses

I II III IV V VI VII VIII IX X

Michael PEARL   Danny BULANADI   Clint CEARLEY

1706 B.C.

DURING A FAMINE, JACOB, WHO WAS ABRAHAM'S GRANDSON, TOOK ELEVEN OF HIS SONS AND ALL THEIR CHILDREN AND SERVANTS DOWN TO EGYPT TO LIVE. IN EGYPT THEY MULTIPLIED LIKE THE DUST OF THE EARTH.

SOON THE SONS OF JACOB, WHOSE NAME WAS CHANGED TO ISRAEL, OUTNUMBERED THE EGYPTIANS.

PHARAOH, THE RULER OF EGYPT, MADE SLAVES OF THE SONS OF JACOB AND FORCED THEM TO DO CRUEL WORK, MAKING BRICKS. AFTER BEING THERE OVER 300 YEARS, THEY HAD FORGOTTEN THE PROMISES GOD MADE TO ABRAHAM AND TO THEIR FATHERS.

GOD HAD TOLD ABRAHAM THAT HIS PEOPLE WOULD GO DOWN TO A STRANGE LAND AND BE SERVANTS THERE. HE ALSO PROMISED THAT AFTER 400 YEARS HE WOULD JUDGE THAT NATION AND BRING HIS PEOPLE BACK INTO THE LAND OF PROMISE.

I TELL YOU IT'S TRUE! PHARAOH FEARS WE ARE BECOMING TOO MANY. HE IS KILLING ALL THE BABIES. THE EGYPTIANS ARE WEAK AND LAZY. OUR MEN ARE STRONG FROM HARD WORK. THEY ARE AFRAID OF US.

THEY ARE NOT GOING TO KILL MY BABY. GOD WILL PROTECT HIM.

HA! WHAT CAN GOD DO AGAINST THE MIGHT OF PHARAOH?

NO! NOT MY BABY. YOU CAN'T DO THIS.

PHARAOH, FEARING THAT THE JEWS WERE BECOMING TOO MANY, DECIDED TO KILL ALL THE NEWBORN MALES.

GENESIS 46:5-7; EXODUS 1:1-12, 22

EXODUS 2:3-9

BUT THEY WILL NOT BELIEVE THAT YOU HAVE SENT ME. THEY WILL JUST LAUGH.

THROW YOUR STAFF ON THE GROUND.

WHAT? MY STAFF!

IT HAS BECOME A DEADLY SERPENT!

PICK UP THE SERPENT BY THE TAIL.

IT HAS TURNED BACK INTO MY ROD!

GO TO EGYPT. I WILL TEACH YOU WHAT TO SAY AND TELL YOU WHAT TO DO. YOUR BROTHER AARON WILL BE YOUR ASSISTANT.

SEE? MY MAGICIANS CAN DO THAT TOO. I WILL NOT BE PERSUADED BY YOUR *MAGIC TRICKS*.

I HAVE NEVER IN MY LIFE SEEN *ANYTHING* LIKE IT. EVEN THE SPRINGS AND LITTLE PONDS HAVE TURNED INTO BLOOD. WHAT DID HE SAY WAS THE NAME OF HIS GOD?

NEVER HEARD THEM SAY. WHAT DIFFERENCE DOES IT MAKE? WE HAVE THOUSANDS OF GODS. THE GOD OF THE NILE RIVER MUST BE ANGRY.

THAT FELLOW MOSES SAYS THAT HIS GOD IS THE ONLY GOD.

ONE GOD? THAT'S *RIDICULOUS*.

SEVEN DAYS AFTER THE WATERS WERE TURNED TO BLOOD, MOSES AGAIN BROUGHT GOD'S JUDGMENTS ON EGYPT.

LET THE WATERS BRING FORTH FROGS IN ABUNDANCE.

THE STINKING BLOOD WATERS SUDDENLY PRODUCED MILLIONS OF FROGS.

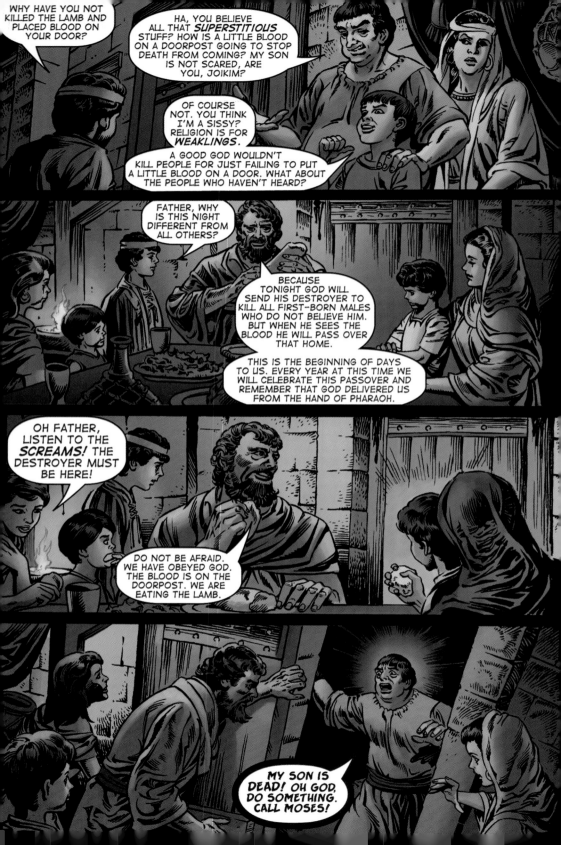

EXODUS 12:29-31

EXODUS

Michael **PEARL**   Danny **BULANADI**   Clint **CEARLEY**

THEY FOLLOWED UNTIL THEY CAME INTO THE MOUNTAINS AND UP AGAINST THE RED SEA. THERE THEY CAMPED WHILE THEY DISCUSSED HOW THEY WERE GOING TO GET ACROSS THE VAST BODY OF WATER.

AFTER PHARAOH GRIEVED FOR HIS CHILD, HIS ANGER INCREASED HOTTER THAN EVER. WHY DID HE LET HIS SLAVES LEAVE?

READY THE CHARIOTS. PURSUE THE HEBREWS. KILL THEM ALL, OR BRING THEM BACK.

IT WILL BE AS YOU SAY, YOUR MAJESTY.

EXODUS 14:5-7

WHEN IT LOOKED AS IF THE EGYPTIAN ARMY WOULD RUSH UPON THE HEBREWS, SUDDENLY A LARGE COLUMN OF FIRE CAME DOWN FROM HEAVEN AND BLOCKED THEIR WAY. DURING THAT NIGHT, THE HEBREWS HAD LIGHT BUT THE EGYPTIANS WERE IN THICK DARKNESS.

MOSES LIFTED HIS STAFF OVER THE SEA AND A GREAT WIND CAME FROM HEAVEN, BLOWING UPON THE SEA, AND THE SEA PARTED, LEAVING A DRY PATH ON THE BOTTOM OF THE SEA FLOOR.

THIS WAS A MOST MAGNIFICENT MIRACLE. THE CHILDREN OF ISRAEL WALKED ACROSS THE SEA ON DRY GROUND.

IN THE FUTURE THEY WOULD SING ABOUT A GOD WHO MADE PATHS IN THE SEA. EVERYONE WOULD KNOW THAT THERE IS BUT ONE GOD AND HIS NAME IS JEHOVAH.

THE WATER FLOWED LIKE A RIVER.

AGAIN THE CLOUD MOVED, AND THE HEBREWS PACKED UP AND FOLLOWED IT INTO THE WILDERNESS TO A MOUNTAIN CALLED SINAI.

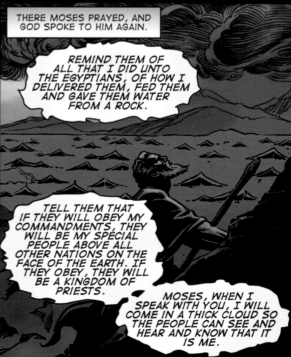

THERE MOSES PRAYED, AND GOD SPOKE TO HIM AGAIN.

REMIND THEM OF ALL THAT I DID UNTO THE EGYPTIANS, OF HOW I DELIVERED THEM, FED THEM AND GAVE THEM WATER FROM A ROCK.

TELL THEM THAT IF THEY WILL OBEY MY COMMANDMENTS, THEY WILL BE MY SPECIAL PEOPLE ABOVE ALL OTHER NATIONS ON THE FACE OF THE EARTH. IF THEY OBEY, THEY WILL BE A KINGDOM OF PRIESTS.

MOSES, WHEN I SPEAK WITH YOU, I WILL COME IN A THICK CLOUD SO THE PEOPLE CAN SEE AND HEAR AND KNOW THAT IT IS ME.

EXODUS 24:9-10

MOSES, YOU WILL HAVE THE PEOPLE BUILD A TABERNACLE IN WHICH TO WORSHIP ME. IT WILL HAVE AN ALTAR ON WHICH TO OFFER SACRIFICES AND A HOLY PLACE WHERE I CAN MEET WITH THE HIGH PRIEST ONCE A YEAR THROUGHOUT ALL YOUR GENERATIONS.

I WILL TELL YOU EXACTLY HOW TO MAKE THE TABERNACLE. THE TRIBE OF LEVI SHALL BE MY PRIESTS, AND AARON, AND HIS SONS AFTER HIM, WILL BE THE HIGH PRIESTS. THEY SHALL TEACH THE PEOPLE TO BE RIGHTEOUS AND THEY WILL OFFER SACRIFICES WHEN THE PEOPLE SIN.

IT WAS *WEEKS* AGO THAT HE DISAPPEARED INTO THE FIRE ON THAT MOUNTAIN. HE MUST BE DEAD BY NOW.

YEAH, WE CAN'T SIT HERE IN THIS WILDERNESS FOREVER.

WE NEED A GOD TO LEAD US AS MOSES DID.

LET US MAKE A GOLDEN IMAGE UNTO OUR GOD.

MOSES IS DEAD. AARON WILL *MAKE* US A GOD OF GOLD TO LEAD US BACK INTO EGYPT.

GIVE US YOUR GOLD.

WITH THEIR OWN HANDS THE FOOLS CREATED A STATUE OF A BULL AND CALLED IT GOD. THE ORIGINAL IMAGE OF SATAN BEFORE HE SINNED WAS THAT OF A BULL. THOUGH THE PEOPLE DIDN'T KNOW IT, SATAN HAD INSPIRED THEM TO WORSHIP HIM.

AARON FOLLOWED THE WISHES OF THE PEOPLE AND HELPED THEM BUILD THE GOD OF GOLD.

EXODUS 20:4; 25:8-9; 28:1-3; 32:1-4; EZEKIEL 1:10; 10:11; 28:14

THE SNAKES EVEN FOUND THEM IN THEIR TENTS AT NIGHT.

HISSSS

GOD HELP US!

SOON THE CAMP WAS FILLED WITH POISONOUS SNAKES.

HELP ME. I HAVE BEEN BITTEN.

NOOOOOO!

NO, JOAB!

MOTHER!

EVEN THE CHILDREN SUFFERED FOR THE SINS OF THEIR PARENTS.

THE PRIESTS ATTENDED TO THE TABERNACLE AND OFFERED DAILY SACRIFICES AS MOSES HAD COMMANDED.

AFTER FORTY YEARS IN THE WILDERNESS, JUST AS EVERYONE ELSE WAS PREPARING TO ENTER INTO THE PROMISED LAND, GOD CALLED MOSES UP INTO THE MOUNTAIN. THERE, AFTER ONE FINAL TALK WITH GOD, HE LAY DOWN AND QUIETLY DIED.

IMMEDIATELY, HIS SPIRIT WAS USHERED INTO THE PRESENCE OF GOD. THERE, HE WAS TO ABIDE UNTIL THE END OF TIME WHEN HE WOULD AGAIN JOIN HIS PEOPLE IN THE LAND GOD HAD PROMISED TO ABRAHAM.

NEARLY *500* YEARS HAD GONE BY SINCE JEHOVAH GOD CALLED ABRAHAM TO LEAVE HIS PEOPLE AND WALK THE LAND GOD WOULD GIVE HIM.

GOD'S PROMISE TO ABRAHAM AND SARAH TO MAKE A GREAT NATION FROM THEIR SON ISAAC WAS FULFILLED. THE TWELVE SONS OF JACOB, WHOSE NAME WAS CHANGED TO ISRAEL, HAD BECOME TWELVE TRIBES AND A MULTITUDE OF PEOPLE.

THEY CAME THROUGH SLAVERY, WANDERED IN THE DESERT WITH MOSES, RECEIVED THE LAW OF GOD, AND NOW AT LAST WERE ENTERING THE *PROMISED LAND*. THROUGHOUT THE WILDERNESS JOURNEY, A YOUNG BOY WAS ALWAYS BESIDE MOSES, WATCHING AND LEARNING HOW TO LEAD THE NATION OF ISRAEL.

THAT BOY GREW UP TO BE THE MIGHTY WARRIOR, *JOSHUA*.

Beauty Queen

The Story of Esther

Ben AVERY   Noval HERNAWAN   Lisa MOORE   Zach MATHENY

HADASSAH! HADASSAH!!!

JERUSHA! HELLO!

HAVE YOU HEARD THE NEWS?

MEIRA'S BEEN BETROTHED!

NO! TO WHO?

I STILL DON'T UNDERSTAND WHAT HAPPENED TO QUEEN VASHTI.

WELL, REMEMBER THAT BIG PARTY A FEW YEARS AGO THAT EVERYONE IN SUSA WAS SUPPOSED TO CELEBRATE?

KING XERXES WAS ACTUALLY PLANNING THOSE BATTLES WITH GREECE THAT THEY ENDED UP LOSING, AND HAD BROUGHT IN ALL HIS MILITARY MEN AND NOBLES AND EVERYONE.

AND QUEEN VASHTI HAD HER OWN PARTY GOING ON, BUT THE KING ORDERED HER TO COME TO HIS.

I HEARD THE REASON SHE DIDN'T GO WAS BECAUSE HE ORDERED HER TO COME AND APPEAR BEFORE EVERYONE WEARING NOTHING BUT HER CROWN!

I THOUGHT I HEARD SOMETHING LIKE THAT. KING OR NOT, I CAN'T IMAGINE HE'D DISRESPECT HER LIKE THAT.

I'VE HEARD SHE WAS QUITE BEAUTIFUL...

WELL, REGARDLESS OF THE DETAILS, THE KING WANTED TO SHOW OFF HER BEAUTY, SHE REFUSED, SO THE KING SENT HER OUT!

DIDN'T HE SEND OUT A DECREE THAT ALL WIVES WERE TO RESPECT THEIR HUSBANDS OR SOMETHING?

YEAH! AND NOW, FOUR YEARS LATER, HE'S LOOKING FOR ANOTHER WIFE!

A BEAUTIFUL WIFE -- THE MOST BEAUTIFUL VIRGIN IN PERSIA IS WHAT I HEARD HE'S LOOKING FOR.

LUCKILY, I'M IN NO DANGER OF BEING SELECTED FOR THAT, SINCE I'M ALREADY MARRIED!

WHO CARES? A GIRL LIKE HER, SHE'S LUCKY TO GET ANYONE!

SPEAKING OF BRIDES, HAVE YOU HEARD WHAT THE KING IS DOING?

YES. YOU'D HAVE TO BE LIVING IN A CAVE NOT TO KNOW.

I'D HATE TO BE THE BRIDE OF KING XERXES, ESPECIALLY CONSIDERING WHAT HAPPENED WITH HIS LAST WIFE!

GIVE MEIRA MY CONGRATULA-TIONS!

WHEN ARE WE GOING TO HEAR THE SAME KIND OF NEWS FOR YOU?

YOU'RE THE LAST OF US, AND YOU'RE SO BEAUTIFUL WE ALL EXPECTED YOU TO BE THE FIRST!

MY COUSIN IS BUSY, HE HASN'T HAD TIME TO LOOK FOR A HUSBAND FOR ME!

HA! HE BETTER NOT WAIT TOO MUCH LONGER!

I THINK KING XERXES WOULD HAVE WON THOSE BATTLES IF THEY'D SPENT MORE TIME PLANNING BATTLES AND LESS TIME DRINKING AND REVELING, EH?

YOU'RE PROBABLY RIGHT.

ONE, PLEASE.

FOR YOUR COUSIN, OF COURSE?

OF COURSE! THEY ARE HIS FAVORITE!

HE IS A LUCKY PERSON, HAVING YOU TO TAKE CARE OF HIM!

YOU'VE GOT IT ALL WRONG; I AM A LUCKY PERSON HAVING HIM TO TAKE CARE OF ME!

MORDECAI!

HADASSAH! WHAT ARE YOU DOING HERE?

JUST HOPING I WOULD CATCH YOU BEFORE YOU LEFT!

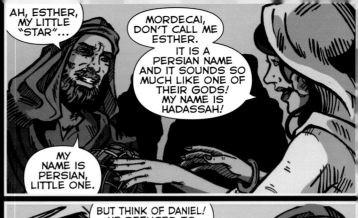

AH, ESTHER, MY LITTLE "STAR"...

MORDECAI, DON'T CALL ME ESTHER. IT IS A PERSIAN NAME AND IT SOUNDS SO MUCH LIKE ONE OF THEIR GODS! MY NAME IS HADASSAH!

MY NAME IS PERSIAN, LITTLE ONE.

BUT THINK OF DANIEL! HE REFUSED TO BE CALLED BALTESHAZZAR!

TRUE. BUT A NAME DOES NOT CHANGE WHO YOU ARE!

YOU'RE RIGHT, COUSIN...

...BUT SO AM I!

OH, HADASSAH, WHAT A JOY YOU ARE, AFTER SUCH A LONG TIME OF SUFFERING!

SUFFERING? WHAT'S WRONG, COUSIN?

WORKING ALL DAY NEAR THAT POMPOUS AGAGITE CALLED HAMAN, THAT'S WHAT! PROMOTION, GETTING AHEAD, ELEVATING HIS STATUS! IT'S ALL HE CARES ABOUT!

ME? I CAN'T PLAY POLITICAL GAMES, I JUST BE MYSELF AND WORK HARD!

THAT'S WHY YOU HAVE ALMOST THE SAME STATUS AS HIM—

YOU! HALT WHERE YOU ARE!

WELCOME, FAIR MAIDENS, TO KING XERXES'S PALACE!

BY NOW, YOU NO DOUBT KNOW WHY YOU ARE HERE!

YOU ARE HERE FOR ONE REASON AND ONE REASON ONLY: TO PLEASE THE KING!

AND WE ARE GOING TO SPEND THE NEXT YEAR TEACHING YOU EXACTLY HOW TO LOOK, SPEAK, AND ACT SO THAT YOU MIGHT ACHIEVE THAT GOAL!

LISTEN AND LEARN, FOR ONE OF YOU WILL, HOPEFULLY, BE CROWNED QUEEN...

...ALL THAT YOU NEED WILL BE BROUGHT TO YOU HERE. JUST ASK ME OR ANY OTHER SERVANT.

AND THIS... THIS MIRROR? WHAT IS IT FOR, SHABNAN?

IF YOU WANT TO MAKE YOURSELF BEAUTIFUL, YOU MUST BE ABLE TO SEE YOURSELF.

HAVE YOU NEVER STOPPED TO ADMIRE YOUR REFLECTION IN A POOL OF WATER? IT IS JUST LIKE THAT.

I HAVE NOT.

I WOULD, WERE I AS BEAUTIFUL AS YOU...

...YOU MUST NOT ONLY LOOK PLEASANT, BUT SMELL PLEASANT. THE SENSE OF SMELL IS ONE OF THE MOST POWERFUL OF OUR SENSES.

EVEN FOR YOU, HEGAI?

I'VE FOUND THAT THE POWER OF SCENT COMES NOT FROM THE SCENT ITSELF, BUT FROM THE MEMORY THE SCENT EVOKES.

FOR ME, WHEN I SMELL THIS LAVENDER, MY HEART TURNS MELANCHOLY AS I THINK OF MY DEAR SWEET MOTHER, BUT OTHER MEN'S THOUGHTS MAY TURN TO...

...IT'S LIKE THE PEACOCK, USING ITS BRIGHT FEATHERS TO ATTRACT A MATE.

THE TRICK IS TO FIND THE BALANCE BETWEEN GETTING ATTENTION AND RETAINING YOUR NATURAL BEAUTY...

...IF YOU APPROACH THE KING WITHOUT HIS PERMISSION, YOU WILL DIE IF HE DOES NOT EXTEND HIS SCEPTER TO YOU!

AND IF THE KING CALLS FOR YOU, YOU WILL DIE IF YOU DO NOT GO TO HIM!

WHAT OF QUEEN VASHTI?

THAT WAS POLITICAL! MAKE NO MISTAKE! NONE OF YOU ARE QUEEN VASHTI...

...YOU'RE REALLY GOING TO WEAVE SOMEONE ELSE'S HAIR INTO YOUR OWN?

THE POOR GIRL THEY BOUGHT IT FROM HAS NO NEED FOR IT.

WITH HAIR LIKE YOURS, YOU'LL NOT WANT ANY WIGS OR EXTENSIONS, YOU LUCKY BRAT.

TOO BAD THEY COULDN'T BUY YOUR HAIR FOR ME...

...TRUE BEAUTY GRACE AND WARMTH, NOT JUST SENSUALITY.

TRULY, I BELIEVE ONLY ONE OF YOU HERE KNOWS WHAT I AM TALKING ABOUT.

ALTHOUGH, I THINK SHE STILL DOESN'T KNOW THAT SHE KNOWS...

...WHY ARE SOME OF THE WOMEN ARE PUTTING ON THE POWDER?

DEAR ESTHER, EVERY WOMAN DOES WHAT THEY BELIEVE WILL MAKE THEM BEAUTIFUL.

FOR MANY, IT MEANS CREATING A MASK TO COVER THEIR TRUE VISAGE.

YOU, MY DEAR, NEED NO MASK...

...OTHER WOMEN WILL CHOOSE TO WEAR MORE REVEALING DRESSES.

THAT COULD SUIT YOUR PHYSICALITY, ESTHER, BUT NOT YOUR PERSONALITY.

HEGAI, SO MANY WOMEN ARE FAR MORE BEAUTIFUL THAN I.

WHY ARE YOU TAKING SUCH AN INTEREST IN ME?

YOU DO NOT UNDERSTAND, DEAR ESTHER, AND THAT MAKES YOU ALL THE MORE BEAUTIFUL...

...YOU MAY ASK FOR WHATEVER YOU WANT TO USE WHEN YOU ARE SUMMONED TO APPEAR BEFORE THE KING.

HOWEVER, I SUGGEST SIMPLE JEWELRY AND ORNAMENTS AND MAKE UP THAT WILL ACCENT YOUR BEAUTY, NOT COVER IT UP.

JUST FOLLOW MY INSTRUCTIONS, NOT THE ADVICE OF THOSE VAIN HENS WHO --

ESTHER!!!

ESTHER! DEAR ESTHER!

WHO IS THAT?

HE IS MORDECAI. HE WORKS AT THE KING'S GATE. HE IS MY COUSIN.

ESTHER, YOU CANNOT SEE HIM. THE KING IS VERY JEALOUS OF HIS WOMEN, AND YOU ARE ESSENTIALLY ONE OF HIS WIVES NOW.

I HAVEN'T SEEN HIM FOR ALMOST A YEAR! SINCE YOUR PEOPLE TOOK ME!

BUT MORDECAI ADOPTED ME! RAISED ME! PROTECTED ME!

AND I AM TO PROTECT YOU NOW!

THAT'S THE BEAUTY OF IT! YOU'LL STILL BE WITH ME!

OH, MORDECAI! MY DEAR COUSIN!

THEY SAID A MAN CAME TO THE HAREM GATE EVERY MORNING, ASKING ABOUT ME!

I KNEW IT WAS YOU!

ARE YOU WELL?

I AM. HEGAI, THE EUNUCH CHARGED WITH CARING FOR US, HAS TAKEN A GREAT INTEREST IN ME.

HE HAS GIVEN ME SEVEN SERVING GIRLS AND THE BEST PLACE IN THE HAREM. AND I...

I HAVE DONE WHAT HE HAS ASKED OF ME. AND WILL CONTINUE TO DO SO.

HER YEAR OF PREPARATION IS FINISHED. SHE WILL BE SUMMONED TO GO BEFORE THE KING SOON.

OH, ESTHER. DO NOT BE AFRAID. WHEN YOU STAND BEFORE THE KING, JUST REMEMBER WHAT I HAVE TOLD YOU.

I AM NOT ALONE.

YOU ARE NEVER ALONE.

WHEN THE TIME COMES, I KNOW YOU WILL LET YOUR TRUE BEAUTY NATURALLY SHINE –

Esther 2:17-18

MY KING, MAY MY WIFE AND I OFFER YOU OUR CONGRATULATIONS?

YOU MAY, HAMAN! YOU MAY!

ESTHER, YOU'RE AS BEAUTIFUL AS THEY SAY.

THANK YOU.

ESTHER!

ESTHER! A WORD!

MY KING, MIGHT YOU EXCUSE ME FOR A MOMENT?

YES, YES, ESTHER! COME BACK SOON!

NOW, HAMAN, I UNDERSTAND YOU HAVE SOME UNIQUE IDEAS!

MORDECAI, I CANNOT BELIEVE WHAT HAS HAPPENED!

IT'S BEEN LIKE A WHIRLWIND AND I'M CAUGHT IN THE MIDDLE OF IT!

I'VE HEARD THE KING HAS EVEN CUT THE TAXES DUE HIM FROM THE PROVINCES AS PART OF THE CELEBRATION!

IT'S ALL SO OVERWHELMING!

MORDECAI, WHAT IS WRONG?

THIS MORNING, WHEN I ARRIVED AT THE KING'S GATE, I OVERHEARD TWO MEN TALKING ANGRILY.

"THEIR NAMES ARE BIGTHAN AND TERESH – SOME OF THE KING'S EUNUCHS. YOU MAY EVEN KNOW.

"THEY MAY HAVE BEEN ANGRY BECAUSE A WOMAN THEY FAVORED WAS NOT NAMED QUEEN.

"AS YOU KNOW, NORMALLY THE KING IS ALMOST COMPLETELY INACCESSIBLE, BUT DURING THESE TIMES OF REVELING, THE KING IS UNIQUELY EXPOSED

"AND I LISTENED TO THEM AS THEY DETAILED THEIR PLANS TO USE THE CHAOS OF THE CELEBRATIONS AND

-- TO KILL THE KING!!!

WHY ARE YOU TELLING ME THIS?

IF THEY SUCCEED, IT WILL PUT THIS WHOLE NATION AND ALL THE SURROUNDING PROVINCES IN A VERY PRECARIOUS SITUATION.

I AM JUST A SINGLE MAN, AND, AS A JEWISH MAN, DESPISED BY MANY, SUCH AS HAMAN.

BUT YOU? YOU ARE THE QUEEN.

TELL ME EVERYTHING.

EVERYTHING.

ESTHER! HAVE YOU MET HAMAN? HE'S A POLITICIAN, MAKE NO MISTAKE, BUT I FIND HIS AMBITION USEFUL.

THANK YOU, MY LORD. MAY YOU LIVE FOREVER.

MY KING, I APOLOGIZE FOR INTERRUPTING, AND I KNOW YOUR TIME IS VALUABLE.

ESTHER, IS SOMETHING WRONG?

MY... I KNOW SOMEONE WHO WORKS AT THE KING'S GATE, AND WHILE THERE HE... HE OVERHEARD TWO MEN TALKING.

WHAT IS IT?

I'M SORRY, HAMAN, I HAVE SOMETHING I MUST ATTEND TO. ESTHER, COME!

PLEASE! WE HAVE NOT DONE ANYTHING!

NO?

MY MEN HAVE DONE A THOROUGH INVESTIGATION! I WANTED TO BE SURE BEFORE PUNISHING SUCH TRUSTED SERVANTS AS YOU! AND I HAVE FOUND THAT YOU INTENDED TO VIOLATE AND USE THAT TRUST TO KILL ME!

ME!!!

AND FOR THAT, YOU WILL DIE!!! YOU WILL BE IMPALED AND THE WORLD WILL SEE YOUR DEATH THROES!!! TAKE

ESTHER, WHO GAVE YOU THIS INFORMATION?

HIS NAME IS MORDECAI.

HIS NAME WILL BE NOTED IN THE ROYAL RECORD, AND HE WILL BE DULY

MILADY, QUEEN ESTHER!

MAY I OFFER YOU SOME FRUIT THIS MORNING?

I USED TO GET THESE FRUITS FOR MY COUSIN WHENEVER WE HAD A SPARE COIN.

AND NOW, LOOK AT ME!

YOUR COUSIN... HE'S THAT MORDECAI WHO WORKS AT THE KING'S GATE, IS HE NOT?

YES. I HAVE MUCH MORE FREEDOM THAN I DID BEFORE, BUT EVER SINCE HAMAN WAS PROMOTED, I'VE SEEN MORDECAI BUT A FEW TIMES.

I THINK KING XERXES FORGOT ABOUT HOW MY COUSIN FOILED THE ASSASSINATION PLOT.

HOW ELSE CAN YOU EXPLAIN THAT HE GAVE HAMAN A PROMOTION LIKE THAT, BUT MY COUSIN REMAINS IN HIS POSITION AT THE KING'S GATE?

AND NOW, HAMAN THINKS JUST BECAUSE HE HAS THE KING'S FAVOR THAT HE CAN ACT LIKE A KING HIM-SELF!

YOUR COUSIN SURE DID PUT A PEBBLE IN HAMAN'S SANDAL, THOUGH!

I MEAN, WHY NOT BOW TO THE MAN?

BECAUSE HE'S... BECAUSE HE...

MILADY ESTHER!

WHAT IS IT, HATHACH?

MILADY, I KNOW YOU ARE FOND OF THE OLDER GENTLEMAN WHO WORKS AT THE KING'S GATE.

AND TODAY I... I SAW HIM OUTSIDE THE KING'S GATE.

WHAT IS UNUSUAL ABOUT THAT?

MY QUEEN, HE WAS OUTSIDE THE KING'S GATE BECAUSE HE WAS NOT ALLOWED ANY FURTHER THAN THAT.

NOT ALLOWED ANY FURTHER? WHAT DO YOU MEAN?

HE WAS CLAD IN SACKCLOTH AND WAS WEEPING, MOURNING WITH ASHES!

AS YOU WELL KNOW, NO ONE WEARING THE CLOTHES OF MOURNERS IS ALLOWED PAST THE KING'S GATE.

SOMETHING TERRIBLE HAS HAPPENED.

I MUST GO AND TEND TO HIM! SOMETHING AWFUL MUST HAVE HAPPENED!

LADY ESTHER, NO! YOU CANNOT GO DOWN THERE! YOU ARE QUEEN, BUT THERE ARE APPEARANCES THAT MUST BE KEPT!

SOMETHING MUST BE DONE! BRING HIM TO ME SO I CAN HELP HIM!

HE CANNOT ENTER IN THOSE CLOTHES!

THEN GO, HATHACH! TAKE HIM SOME CLOTHES AND BRING HIM HERE! LET HIM KNOW THAT WHATEVER IS WRONG, I WILL FIX IT FOR HIM!

HATHACH, WHERE IS MORDECAI?

GOOD QUEEN, I BEG YOUR MERCY. I TOOK HIM THE CLOTHES, AS YOU ORDERED ME TO.

AND?

HE REFUSES TO TAKE OFF THE SACKCLOTH? WHAT TERRIBLE THING HAS HAPPENED, THAT HE CANNOT STOP HIS MOURNING TO COME TO ME?!?

HATHACH! YOU MUST GO BACK TO HIM AND FIND OUT WHAT IS WRONG!

"HAMAN'S DISLIKE FOR MORDECAI IS NOT MERELY FROM PRIDE AND POLITICS, BUT FROM GENERATIONS OF HATRED TOWARD YOUR PEOPLE.

"THE RAGE THAT BURNED IN HAMAN'S HEART WAS SUCH THAT HE DID NOT JUST SEEK TO DESTROY MORDECAI, HE CAST LOTS AS HE SOUGHT THE LUCKIEST DAY TO KILL YOUR ENTIRE PEOPLE!

"HE CAST A LOT FOR EACH MONTH AND EACH TIME, IT WAS DETERMINED TO BE UNLUCKY, UNTIL HE ARRIVED TO THE TWELFTH MONTH.

"THE KING GAVE HAMAN THE ROYAL SIGNET RING AND GAVE HIM PERMISSION TO WRITE A DECREE CALLING FOR THE JEWS' DESTRUCTION.

"THE DATE DETERMINED BY LOT: THE THIRTEENTH DAY OF ADAR.

"THEN, HE WENT BEFORE KING XERXES AND SAID THAT THE JEWISH PEOPLE DO NOT KEEP THE KING'S LAWS.

"HE SUGGESTED THAT IT WOULD BE BEST TO DESTROY THEM, RATHER THAN TO TOLERATE THEM.

"AND ANY WHO HELP ERADICATE THE JEWISH PEOPLE WILL BE GIVEN PERMISSION TO PLUNDER THEIR BELONGINGS.

"NOT JUST IN PERSIA, BUT ALL THE PROVINCES KING XERXES RULES.

"THIS DECREE MEANS ANNIHILATION OF THE FOLLOWERS OF YOUR ONE GOD, AND NOW EVERYWHERE THE JEWS MOURN AND LAMENT.

"AND HE OFFERED THE KING TEN THOUSAND TALENTS – 400 TONS! – OF SILVER FOR THE ROYAL TREASURY.

"YOUR COUSIN AMONG THEM.

"WHILE KING XERXES AND HAMAN SIT DOWN TO DRINK TOGETHER."

THIS CANNOT BE TRUE...

MANY DO NOT BELIEVE THIS DECREE, PERSIANS AND JEWS ALIKE. BUT ALL DISBELIEF VANISHES UPON SEEING IT, SO YOUR COUSIN WANTED ME TO GIVE THIS TO YOU.

IT... IT *IS* TRUE.

YES.

YOUR COUSIN ASKED ME TO GIVE YOU A REQUEST: HE WANTS YOU TO GO TO THE KING.

AND BEG THE KING TO RESCIND THE DECREE.

NO!!!

HE KNOWS THAT IF ANYONE APPROACHES THE KING WITHOUT THE KING'S SUMMONS THAT HE WILL BE PUT TO DEATH!

I AM NO EXCEPTION!

IF I GO BEFORE HIM AND HE DOES NOT EXTEND HIS SCEPTER TO ME, I WILL DIE!

YOU TELL HIM THAT HE ASKS ME TO GO TO MY DEATH!!!

GO! TELL HIM!

ASK HIM HOW HE COULD ASK SUCH OF THING OF ME!!!

Esther

YOU HAVE SPOKEN WITH MORDECAI.

WHAT DID HE SAY?

HE SAID, QUEEN ESTHER, YOU SHOULD NOT THINK YOU COULD ESCAPE HAMAN'S DECREE IN THE PALACE.

YOU MAY AVOID DEATH BY AVOIDING THE KING'S WRATH IF YOU DO NOT APPROACH THE KING.

BUT IF YOU KEEP SILENT, DELIVERANCE WILL STILL COME TO THE JEWS.

BUT YOUR FATHER'S HOUSE WILL PERISH.

AND HE SAID, "FOR WHO KNOWS WHETHER OR NOT YOU HAVE BEEN PLACED IN XERXES KINGDOM --

"--FOR SUCH A TIME AS THIS?"

HATHACH, RETURN TO MORDECAI. TELL HIM THAT ALL JEWS IN SUSA SHOULD PRAY AND FAST FOR ME, FOR THREE DAYS.

MY MAIDS AND I WILL ALSO OBSERVE THIS FAST.

AFTER THOSE THREE DAYS, I WILL GO BEFORE THE KING.

YES, MY QUEEN.

AND IF I PERISH...

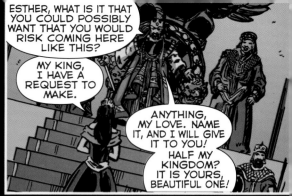

ESTHER! THE KING HAS ARRIVED! AND HAMAN, WITH HIS ESCORT OF KING'S EUNUCHS!

HOW DO I LOOK?

ENTRANCING, AS ALWAYS, MY QUEEN!

MY QUEEN, A MOMENT!

I DO NOT HAVE A MOMENT, HATHACH.

THE KING IS HERE.

WHAT WAS IT, HATHACH?

ONE OF MY COLLEAGUES, HARBONA, GAVE ME SOME DISTURBING NEWS.

HAMAN, AFTER TODAY'S EMBARRASSMENT BY MORDECAI, DOES NOT WANT TO WAIT UNTIL THE MONTH OF ADAR.

HE HAS BUILT A GALLOWS, SEVENTY-FIVE FEET HIGH, WHICH HE INTENDS TO HANG MORDECAI UPON TODAY!

PERHAPS IT IS BEST SHE DOES NOT KNOW.

I DO NOT KNOW WHAT SHE HAS PLANNED, BUT I THINK THE MOTIVATION OF RESCUING HER PEOPLE IS ENOUGH.

ADDING THE PERSONAL THREAT AGAINST HER COUSIN MIGHT JUST THROW HER OFF.

I WAS JUST SPEAKING TO MY WIFE ABOUT THE HONOR YOU HAVE SHOWN ME!

YES, I'VE BEEN CURIOUS ABOUT WHY YOU HAVE CHOSEN TO SO HONOR... US.

THE HONOR OF YOUR PRESENCE IS MINE, DEAR KING XERXES.

WHAT IS IT YOU DESIRE, ESTHER?

NAME IT! IT'S YOURS! EVEN HALF MY KINGDOM!

THE END

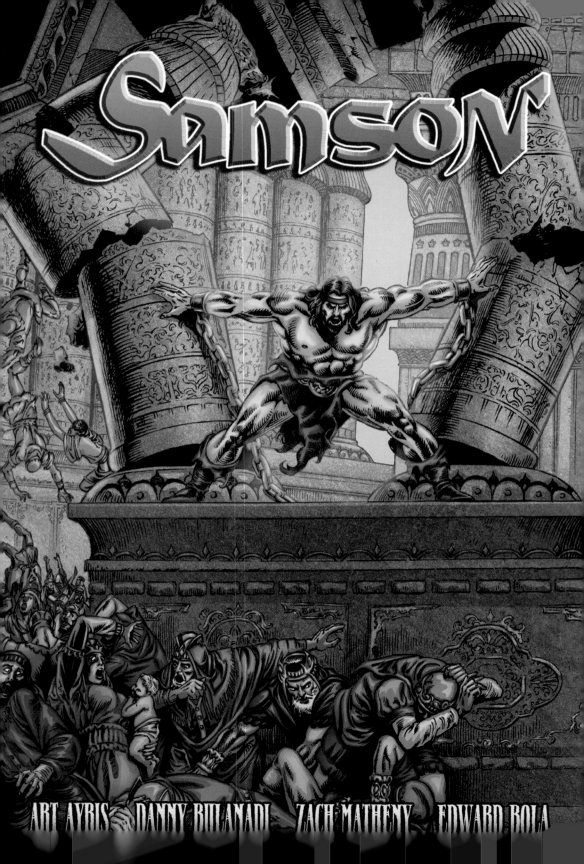

MOSES, THE SERVANT OF GOD WHO LED THE ISRAELITES TO WHOLE-HEARTEDLY FOLLOW GOD HAS PASSED FROM THE SCENE.

AFTER HIM CAME HIS SERVANT JOSHUA. BUT NOW 250 YEARS HAVE PASSED SINCE JOSHUA LED THE PEOPLE OF ISRAEL.

IN EACH GENERATION, AS THE ISRAELITES TURNED FROM FOLLOWING GOD, HE TURNED THEM OVER AS PLUNDER TO THEIR ENEMIES.

GOD HELP US!

BUT EACH TIME THEY WOULD CRY OUT AND HE WOULD SEND A DELIVERER – A JUDGE.

A PEOPLE GROUP LIVING NEARBY – THE PHILISTINES – WERE ETHNICALLY RELATED TO THE EGYPTIANS.

THEY HAD BEEN A PEOPLE OF THE SEA BUT SETTLED IN FIVE CITIES IN CANAAN.

THEY WERE VERY WARLIKE AND WELL KNOWN AS EXPERTS IN IRON SMITHING.

WHEN GOD BROUGHT THE PEOPLE OUT OF THE LAND OF EGYPT HE KEPT THEM FROM GOING THROUGH PHILISTINE TERRITORY EVEN THOUGH THE WAY WAS SHORTER –

"IF THEY FACE WAR, THEY MIGHT CHANGE THEIR MINDS AND RETURN TO EGYPT."

IN 1425 B.C. THE PHILISTINES SUBJUGATED THE PEOPLE OF ISRAEL AND HELD ABSOLUTE RULE OVER THEM FOR 40 YEARS.

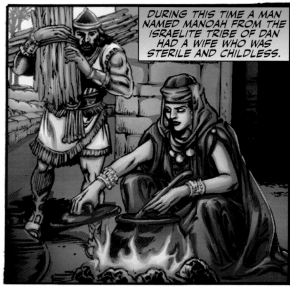

DURING THIS TIME A MAN NAMED MANOAH FROM THE ISRAELITE TRIBE OF DAN HAD A WIFE WHO WAS STERILE AND CHILDLESS.

EXODUS 13:17 - JUDGES 13:1-2

JUDGES 13:3-5

HIS WIFE SHARED WITH HIM ABOUT THE DIVINE ENCOUNTER.

O LORD, I BEG YOU, LET THE MAN OF GOD YOU SENT TO US COME AGAIN TO TEACH US HOW TO BRING UP THE BOY WHOM IS TO BE BORN.

GOD HEARD MANOAH, AND THE ANGEL OF GOD CAME AGAIN BUT MANOAH WAS NOT WITH HIS WIFE.

HE'S HERE! THE MAN WHO APPEARED TO ME THE OTHER DAY!

ARE YOU THE ONE WHO TALKED TO MY WIFE?

I AM.

WHEN YOUR WORDS ARE FULFILLED, WHAT IS TO BE THE RULE FOR THE BOY'S LIFE AND WORK?

JUDGES 13:6-14

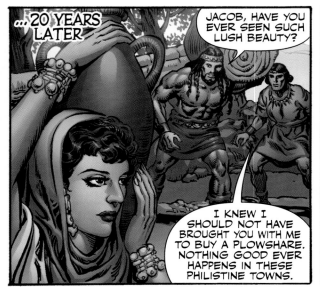

ONE DAY WHILE ON HIS WAY TO VISIT THE PHILISTINES...

HE WAS ATTACKED BY A LION.

BUT WITH HIS GREAT STRENGTH...

...HE KILLED THE LION.

SAMSON WENT AGAIN TO TIMNAH TO TALK WITH THE WOMAN, AND HE LIKED HER.

SHE HAS OUR PERMISSION TO MARRY.

BUT THE MARRIAGE MUST TAKE PLACE HERE, AMONG OUR PEOPLE.

JUST THE MAN I HAVE BEEN LOOKING FOR.

JUDGES 14:5-7

OKAY, WE WILL GO THE WEDDING.

WE ARE NOT SUPPOSED TO INTERMARRY WITH THESE IDOLATERS BUT WE CAN TELL YOU HAVE MADE UP YOUR MIND TO DO SO.

YOU MAY GO TO TIMNAH TO PREPARE THE WEDDING FEAST. WE WILL JOIN YOU IN A DAY OR SO.

ON HIS WAY TO TIMNAH OF THE PHILISTINES...

...HE FOUND THAT THE DEAD LION NOW HAD BEES AND HONEY IN ITS CARCASS.

YUMMM...

NO SENSE IN LETTING GOOD FOOD GO TO WASTE.

* SAMSON'S CONTACT WITH THE DEAD LION WAS A VIOLATION OF HIS NAZIRITE VOW.

MY SON, YOU HAVE LOCATED SOME *VERY* SWEET HONEY.

JUDGES 14:8-9

IT WAS CUSTOMARY AT THE TIME FOR BRIDE-GROOMS TO THROW A FEAST FOR THE MARRIAGE.

* HEBREW WORD MISHTEH – A PARTY THAT ESPECIALLY INCLUDES ALCOHOL, ANOTHER VIOLATION OF HIS NAZIRITE VOW.

THE PHILISTINES PROVIDED 30 PHILISTINE MEN FOR THE OCCASION.

LET ME TELL YOU A RIDDLE.

IF YOU CAN GIVE ME THE ANSWER WITHIN THE SEVEN DAYS OF THE FEAST, I WILL GIVE YOU THIRTY LINEN GARMENTS AND THIRTY SETS OF CLOTHES.

IF YOU CAN'T TELL ME THE ANSWER, YOU MUST GIVE ME THIRTY LINEN GARMENTS AND THIRTY SETS OF CLOTHES.

TELL US YOUR RIDDLE.

LET'S HEAR IT.

OUT OF THE EATER, SOME-THING TO EAT; OUT OF THE STRONG, SOMETHING SWEET.

...SOMETHING SWEET.

THIS HEBREW HAS OUTFOXED US.

FOR FOUR DAYS THE PHILISTINES STRUGGLED AND COULD NOT COME UP WITH THE ANSWER TO THE RIDDLE.

THAT HEBREW COMES HERE AND MAKES A FOOL OF US.

MAYBE WE CAN MAKE A FOOL OF HIM.

JUDGES 14:10-14

MY LADY, THE LORDS OF THE PHILISTINES HAVE REQUESTED TO MEET WITH YOU.

ME?!

COAX YOUR HEBREW LOVER TO TELL YOU THE ANSWER TO THIS STUPID RIDDLE OF HIS.

WE ARE NOT ASKING... WE ARE TELLING YOU.

WE WILL NOT HAVE THIS FOREIGNER COMING IN AND MAKING GOATS OF US.

...NOR ROBBING US.

I CAN'T... HE HAS TOLD NO ONE, NOT EVEN ME.

EITHER HE EXPLAINS THE RIDDLE TO YOU... OR WE WILL BURN YOU AND YOUR FATHER'S HOUSEHOLD TO DEATH. THOSE ARE YOUR OPTIONS.

SOB... SOB

YOU HATE ME! YOU DON'T REALLY LOVE ME. YOU'VE GIVEN MY PEOPLE A RIDDLE, BUT YOU HAVEN'T TOLD ME THE ANSWER.

I HAVEN'T EVEN EXPLAINED IT TO MY FATHER OR MOTHER, SO WHY SHOULD I EXPLAIN IT TO YOU?

...SO SAMSON GAVE IN AND TOLD HER THE ANSWER TO THE RIDDLE.

JUDGES 14:15-17

THE LAST DAY OF THE WEDDING BANQUET.

WHAT IS SWEETER THAN HONEY?

WHAT IS STRONGER THAN A LION?

IF YOU HAD NOT PLOWED WITH MY HEIFER, YOU WOULD NOT HAVE SOLVED MY RIDDLE.

NEVERTHELESS YOU WILL HAVE YOUR 30 GARMENTS.

THE REST OF THAT DAY AND EVENING SAMSON WENT THROUGHOUT THE AREA BEATING AND ROBBING PHILISTINE MEN AND TAKING THEIR FINE ROBES — UNTIL HE HAD ACQUIRED THE 30 SETS.

AAARGHH!

YEOWWW!

A MONSTER!

WHAT THE...

MY DEBT IS PAID.

IN ANGER SAMSON STORMED AWAY AND RETURNED TO HIS FATHER'S HOUSE.

JUDGES 14:18-19

WHO DID THIS??!!!

IT WAS THE ISRAELITE SAMSON – THE ONE PLEDGED TO THE TIMNITE'S DAUGHTER.

HE DID THIS BECAUSE THE WIFE HE HAD BEEN PROMISED WAS GIVEN TO HIS FRIEND.

THIS YOUNG MAN SAW HIM LEAVING THE CITY WALKING INTO THE HILL AREA WHERE ALL THE FOX DENS ARE LOCATED.

LET US OUT – LET US OUT!

EEEAAIYAH!!

HELP US – HAVE MERCY!

NOW, LET'S SEE WHAT SAMSON HAS TO SAY.

YIAHHH!

SAMSON VICIOUSLY ATTACKED THE PHILSTINES IN SURPRISE RAIDS, SLAUGHTERING MANY.

AFTER TAKING REVENGE FOR THE KILLING OF HIS PLEDGED WIFE'S FAMILY HE WENT AND STAYED IN A CAVE IN THE ROCK OF ETAN.

TAKING NO CHANCES THE PHILISTINE RULERS SENT AN ARMY OF FOOT SOLDERS TO RETRIEVE SAMSON AND BRING HIM BACK FOR JUSTICE.

WHY HAVE YOU BROUGHT OUT THIS GREAT ARMY TO FIGHT US?

OUR QUARREL IS NOT WITH YOU. WE HAVE COME TO TAKE SAMSON PRISONER.

WE WILL DO TO HIM AS HE HAS DONE TO US.

WE WILL DO WHAT WE CAN TO DELIVER HIM INTO YOUR HANDS.

GOOD — THAT IS ALL THAT WE SEEK... THIS TIME.

DON'T YOU REALIZE THAT THE PHILISTINES ARE RULERS OVER US?

WHAT HAVE YOU DONE TO US?

THEY HAVE ALREADY TAKEN OUR WEAPONS — THEY WILL KILL US.

I MERELY DID TO THEM WHAT THEY HAD DONE TO ME.

THE ISRAELITES DID NOT REALIZE THAT THOUGH THE PHILISTINES HAD TAKEN THEIR SWORDS AND SPEARS — GOD HAD GIVEN THEM A GREATER WEAPON IN SAMSON.

JUDGES 15:9-11

WE'RE SORRY BUT STILL, WE'VE COME TO TIE YOU UP AND HAND YOU OVER TO THE PHILISITINES.

WE HAVE NO CHOICE – WE HAVE TO DO THIS FOR THE SAKE OF OUR PEOPLE – AND TO PROTECT OUR FAMILIES. OTHER-WISE THE PHILISITINES WILL KILL ALL OF US UNLESS THEY FIND YOU.

JUST SWEAR TO ME THAT YOU WON'T KILL ME YOURSELVES.

AGREED.

WE WILL ONLY TIE YOU UP AND HAND YOU OVER TO THEM. WE WILL NOT KILL YOU.

SO THEY BOUND HIM WITH TWO NEW ROPES...

... AND LED HIM UP FROM THE ROCK.

YIHHHH!

KILL HIM!!

IT'S SAMSON – TAKE HIM ALIVE!

YES – SO WE CAN KILL HIM SLOWLY!

WITH A DONKEY'S JAW-BONE I HAVE MADE DONKEYS OF THEM.

WITH A DONKEY'S JAW-BONE I HAVE KILLED A THOUSAND MEN.

THE PLACE WAS CALLED RAMATH LEHI—JAWBONE KILL.

HE WASN'T A MAN – HE WAS A DEMON!

HE KILLED THE MEN 3-4 AT A TIME.

WE COULDN'T GET TO HIM. THE DEAD BECAME A WALL AROUND HIM. OUR SPEARS WOULD JUST KILL OUR OWN MEN.

THIS RENEGADE LION MUST BE HUNTED DOWN AND KILLED.

MY LORDS – LEAVE HIM BE – DON'T CURSE OUR LAND ANYMORE. LET NO MORE PHILISTINES BE SACRIFICED TO THIS HEBREW GOD THAT SURROUNDS SAMSON.

AND SO GOD AGAIN BROUGHT DELIVERANCE FROM THE PHILISTINES.

JUDGES 15:16-19

AFTER HIS GREAT VICTORY AGAINST THE PHILISITINES SAMSON BECAME THE LEADER OF THE ISRAELITES...

... AND HE LED THEM FOR TWENTY YEARS.

... BUT HIS LUST FOR FORBIDDEN FRUIT WAS NOT SATISFIED. IN DIRECT DISOBEDIENCE TO GOD, HE TRAVELED TO GAZA OF THE PHILISTINES LOOKING FOR SIN.

GOD'S WORD CLEARLY STATES "DO NOT LET YOUR HEART TURN TO HER WAYS OR STRAY INTO HER PATHS.

"MANY ARE THE VICTIMS SHE HAS BROUGHT DOWN; HER SLAIN ARE A MIGHTY THRONG."

"HER HOUSE IS A HIGHWAY TO THE GRAVE, LEADING DOWN TO THE CHAMBERS OF DEATH."

JUDGES 15:20 - PROVERBS 7:25-27

SAMSON IS *HERE* – IN OUR CITY! JERUB THE MILLER SAW HIM ENTER THE HOUSE OF THE PROSTITUTE WHO LIVES BY THE WEAVERS' MARKET.

GOOD. WE DON'T EVEN HAVE TO GO AFTER HIM THIS TIME. OUR GODS HAVE BROUGHT HIM HERE TO US.

WE WILL WAIT UNTIL DAWN AND THEN WE WILL JUMP HIM AS HE COMES OUT OF THE HOUSE – IT WILL TAKE ALL OF US.

HE TOOK HOLD OF THE DOORS OF THE CITY GATE, TOGETHER WITH THE TWO POSTS, AND TORE THEM LOOSE, BAR AND ALL.

HE LIFTED THEM TO HIS SHOULDERS AND CARRIED THEM...

...TO THE TOP OF THE HILL THAT FACED THE CITY.

HE CANNOT BE HUMAN.

...OR MAYBE HIS GOD TRULY IS THE STRONG AND MIGHTY GOD.

WHATEVER HE IS... MAN OR GOD... HE MUST BE STOPPED.

THEY DON'T MAKE LADIES LIKE THIS BACK ON THE FARM.

YOU CAN SAY THAT AGAIN.

LET'S FIND OUT MORE ABOUT THEM.

WELL, LOOK WHAT THE DOGS DRUG IN.

FARM BOYS, THEY'RE NOT FROM AROUND HERE.

YOU NEED TO BLINK YOUR EYES... THEY ARE MEN, ESPECIALLY THE ONE IN THE MIDDLE.

SOMETHING WE CAN HELP YOU WITH?

WE JUST SOLD OUR GRAIN AND SAW THE FESTIVAL, WANTED TO MEET SOME OF THE LOCALS.

AND THIS LOOKED LIKE A GOOD PLACE TO START.

SO, DID THE PHILISTINE MEN GIVE YOU A FAIR PRICE FOR THE GRAIN?

NO, BUT NEITHER DID WE GIVE THEM THE CORRECT WEIGHT. WE KNOW THE PHILISTINE BUYERS ALWAYS TRY TO LOWER OUR PRICES.

GUESS YOU COULD CALL IT A MUTUAL UNDER-STANDING.

YOU ARE WISE.

JUST CALL IT EXPERIENCED.

SHAGOL AND SOME OF THE RULERS WOULD LIKE TO HAVE A WORD WITH YOU...

IT IS TRUE – THE VALLEY OF SOREK PRODUCES SOME OF THE MOST BEAUTIFUL FRUIT IN THE LAND OF THE PHILISTINES.

AND LUSCIOUS...

HOWEVER, WE ARE NOT HERE TO ADMIRE YOUR BEAUTY. WE ARE HERE TO HIRE IT.

YOU HAVE BEEN ABLE TO DO SOMETHING A SQUAD OF 1,000 OF OUR FINEST FOOT SOLDIERS WERE NOT ABLE TO DO – TAME SAMSON.

WE KNOW HE SPENT THE NIGHT AT YOUR HOME A FEW NIGHTS AGO.

SAMSON IS NO MORE TAME THAN THE LIONS THAT ROAM IN THE MOUNTAINS RINGING OUR VALLEY.

BUT AT LEAST HE CAME DOWN FROM THE MOUNTAINS THAT WE COULD SEE HIM.

WE WILL PAY YOU TO TAME HIM.

IT IS DANGEROUS TO TAME WILD ANIMALS. YOU KNOW THE TRAINERS ARE SOME-TIMES KILLED.

WE ARE WILLING TO MAKE IT WORTH THE RISK.

WHAT RISK – WHAT MAN WOULDN'T WILLINGLY GO TO DELILAH'S ARMS?

HOW MUCH?

IF YOU SUBDUE SAMSON AND DELIVER HIM INTO OUR HANDS YOU WILL GET 1100 PIECES OF SILVER...

...FROM EACH OF US.

JUDGES 16:5

WHY ARE YOU UPSET – I'M THE ONE THE PHILISTINES TRIED TO ATTACK.

MEN – YOU KNOW NOTHING!

I KNOW ENOUGH THAT I WANT TO KEEP MY HEAD ON MY SHOULDERS.

SAMSON, WOMEN WANT INTIMACY. WE WANT OUR MEN TO SHARE THEIR SECRETS – THEIR HEARTS WITH US.

HOW CAN WE BE CLOSE IF YOU ARE NOT HONEST WITH ME ABOUT HOW YOU CAN BE TIED.

IF WE ARE GOING TO BE CLOSE WE HAVE TO SHARE EVERY-THING WITH EACH OTHER.

I WILL TELL YOU THE SECRET OF MY GREAT STRENGTH. IF ANYONE TIES ME SECURELY WITH NEW ROPES THAT HAVE NEVER BEEN USED I'LL BECOME AS WEAK AS ANY OTHER MAN.

NOW, YOU HAVE MY HEART...

LET'S GO DRINK DEEPLY OF LOVE, I REALLY FEEL *CLOSE* TO YOU.

...BUT SAMSON SNAPPED THE ROPES LIKE THREADS.

DON'T CRY – LISTEN I HAVE TOLD *NO* ONE.

IS THAT WHAT I AM TO YOU – NO ONE!!!

IF YOU *TRULY* LOVED ME – THERE WOULD BE NO SECRETS BETWEEN US.

SHE NAGGED AND PRODDED HIM EVERY DAY...

...UNTIL HE WAS TIRED TO *DEATH*.

NO RAZOR HAS EVER BEEN USED ON MY HEAD BECAUSE I HAVE BEEN A NAZIRITE SET APART TO GOD SINCE BIRTH.

IF MY HEAD WERE SHAVED, MY STRENGTH WOULD LEAVE ME, AND I WOULD BECOME AS WEAK AS ANY OTHER MAN.

DELILAH KNEW HE HAD TOLD HER EVERYTHING AND SHE SLYLY SENT FOR THE PHILISTINE RULERS.

COME BACK ONCE MORE; HE HAS TOLD ME EVERYTHING.

THIS *BETTER* BE IT.

JUDGES 16:15-18

IT'S BEEN A LONG DAY, WHY DON'T YOU GO TO SLEEP. HERE IN MY LAP, MY LOVE. WHERE IT IS COMFORTABLE.

I REALLY SHOULD BE...

...GOING.

GOING, GOING, GONE... AND MAY IT BE FOR A LONG TIME

HIS HAIR — THE SYMBOL OF GOD'S GREAT STRENGTH IN SAMSON — LEAVES HIM AS DELILAH SHEARS HIM.

THE GREAT LION HAS BECOME A WEAK LAMB.

I'LL GO OUT AS BEFORE AND SHAKE MYSELF FREE.

THE PHILISTINES ARE UPON YOU!

BUT SAMSON DID NOT KNOW THAT THE LORD HAD LEFT HIM BECAUSE OF HIS DISOBEDIENCE.

JUDGES 16: 19-20

WHAAA...?!

BRING HIM TO THIS SUPPORT.

OKAY HEBREW DOG, WE HAVE SEEN WHAT YOU HAVE DONE TO OUR PEOPLE - NOW YOU *WON'T* SEE!

YIAHHHHH....!!!

ENJOY YOUR REWARD DELILAH.

MY REWARD IS SEEING THIS HEBREW DONKEY NO LONGER A SCOURGE TO OUR PEOPLE.

THE ONLY *SCOURGE* SAMSON WILL KNOW NOW IS THE *SCOURGE* OF THE MASTER'S WHIP. THERE HE WILL BE THE *DONKEY* THAT TURNS THE MILL.

JUDGES 16:20-21

BUT WITH THE LOSS OF SIGHT, SAMSON FOR THE FIRST TIME BEGINS TO SEE.

YAHWEH, YOU GAVE ME A GIFT...AND I SQUANDERED IT.

FORGIVE ME.

BUT SAMSON'S HAIR BEGAN TO GROW BACK.

BUT EVEN MORE IMPORTANT — OBEDIENCE RETURNED, AND HIS SPIRIT BEGAN TO COME BACK.

HEAR MY PRAYER O GOD, USE ME YET AGAIN.

I HAVE FALLEN... PICK ME UP.

AND MAKE ME STRONG AGAIN... FOR *YOU*.

GIVE ME ONE MORE CHANCE...

...TO DO YOUR WILL.

JUDGES 16:22

JUDGES 16:22-25

OUR GOD HAS DELIVERED OUR ENEMY INTO OUR HANDS, THE ONE WHO HAS LAID WASTE OUR LAND AND MULTIPLIED OUR SLAIN.

WHERE IS YOUR GOD NOW, SAMSON?!

YOU ARE PATHETIC. I THOUGHT SURELY YOU WOULD GIVE THE PEOPLE A REAL SHOW.

TAKE SAMSON ASIDE.

AFTER THE GAMES WE'LL BRING HIM OUT AGAIN FOR SPORT.

PLEASE DO ME A FAVOR.

AND WHAT IS THAT?

PUT ME WHERE I CAN FEEL THE PILLARS THAT SUPPORT THE TEMPLE, SO THAT I MAY LEAN AGAINST THEM.

O SOVEREIGN LORD, REMEMBER ME.

O GOD, PLEASE STRENGTHEN ME JUST ONCE MORE, AND LET ME WITH ONE BLOW GET REVENGE ON THE PHILISTINES FOR MY TWO EYES.

LET ME DIE WITH THE PHILISTINES.

JUDGES 16:30

THEN HIS BROTHERS AND HIS FATHER'S WHOLE FAMILY WENT DOWN TO GET HIM.

"DO NOT BE DECEIVED. GOD IS NOT MOCKED.

A MAN REAPS WHAT HE SOWS."

THEY BURIED HIM IN THE TOMB OF HIS FATHER, MANOAH.

JUDGES 16:31

SAMSON LED ISRAEL FOR TWENTY YEARS.

"... SHE SEDUCED HIM WITH HER SMOOTH TALK... LITTLE KNOWING IT WILL COST HIM HIS LIFE."

JUDGES 16:31 - PROVERBS 7:21-23

ELIJAH

Michael **PEARL** Danny **BULANADI** Clint **CEARLEY**

JEZEBEL WAS KNOWN FOR HER RELIGIOUS ZEAL. SHE DESPISED THE GOD OF ISRAEL AND PROMOTED BAAL WORSHIP THROUGHOUT THE LAND.

THERE WAS A WEAK MAN NAMED AHAB THAT CAME TO THE THRONE OF ISRAEL, THE NORTHERN HALF OF THE KINGDOM (918 B.C.). HE LIVED UP IN SAMARIA CLOSE TO THE ZIDONIANS. THE ZIDONIANS WERE BAAL WORSHIPERS. AHAB MARRIED JEZEBEL, ONE OF THE DAUGHTERS OF THE PRIESTS OF BAAL.

FIND ALL THE PROPHETS OF JEHOVAH AND *KILL* THEM. *BAAL* WILL BE OUR GOD.

THE KING HAD A SERVANT NAMED OBADIAH WHO WORSHIPED JEHOVAH.

I MUST FIND THE PROPHETS OF GOD AND WARN THEM.

OBADIAH HID 100 PROPHETS IN A CAVE AND BROUGHT THEM FOOD AND WATER.

1 KINGS 16:28, 31, 18:4

1 KINGS 17:1, 10-16

I HAD THEM ALL KILLED. THEY WERE *LIARS* AND *DECEIVERS*.

YOU WHAT? YOU *IDIOT!* YOU SHOULD HAVE *KILLED ELIJAH!*

BUT HIS GOD ANSWERED BY FIRE. IT WAS A *MIRACLE.* OUR PRIESTS WERE *POWERLESS.* THE PEOPLE ALL TURNED TO JEHOVAH.

BUT, HONEY, WHAT ELSE COULD I DO? I *FEARED* THE PEOPLE!

YOU KILLED MY PRIESTS. *YOU FOOL!*

NO MIRACLE WILL PROTECT ELIJAH FROM THE WRATH OF BAAL.

IF I DO NOT KILL ELIJAH FOR THIS, LET THE GODS DO THE *SAME* TO ME AND MORE.

I MUST GET AWAY.

ELIJAH FORGOT TO TRUST GOD AND FLED FOR HIS LIFE.

1 KINGS 19:1-4

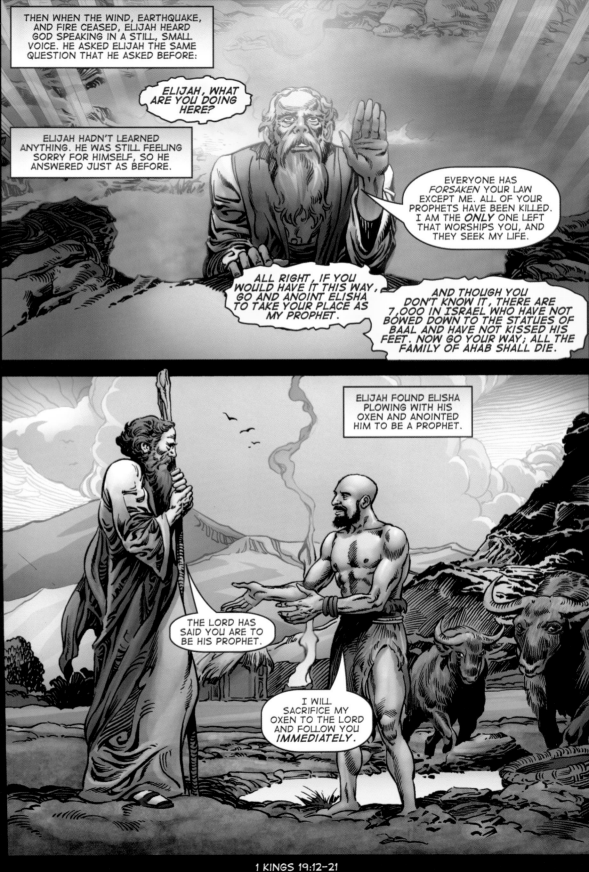

THEN WHEN THE WIND, EARTHQUAKE, AND FIRE CEASED, ELIJAH HEARD GOD SPEAKING IN A STILL, SMALL VOICE. HE ASKED ELIJAH THE SAME QUESTION THAT HE ASKED BEFORE:

ELIJAH, WHAT ARE YOU DOING HERE?

ELIJAH HADN'T LEARNED ANYTHING. HE WAS STILL FEELING SORRY FOR HIMSELF, SO HE ANSWERED JUST AS BEFORE.

EVERYONE HAS FORSAKEN YOUR LAW EXCEPT ME. ALL OF YOUR PROPHETS HAVE BEEN KILLED. I AM THE ONLY ONE LEFT THAT WORSHIPS YOU, AND THEY SEEK MY LIFE.

ALL RIGHT, IF YOU WOULD HAVE IT THIS WAY, GO AND ANOINT ELISHA TO TAKE YOUR PLACE AS MY PROPHET.

AND THOUGH YOU DON'T KNOW IT, THERE ARE 7,000 IN ISRAEL WHO HAVE NOT BOWED DOWN TO THE STATUES OF BAAL AND HAVE NOT KISSED HIS FEET. NOW GO YOUR WAY; ALL THE FAMILY OF AHAB SHALL DIE.

ELIJAH FOUND ELISHA PLOWING WITH HIS OXEN AND ANOINTED HIM TO BE A PROPHET.

THE LORD HAS SAID YOU ARE TO BE HIS PROPHET.

I WILL SACRIFICE MY OXEN TO THE LORD AND FOLLOW YOU IMMEDIATELY.

1 KINGS 19:12-21

RIGHT NEXT TO AHAB'S PALACE WAS A VINEYARD OWNED BY NABOTH. AHAB OFTEN LOOKED OUT THE WINDOW AND ADMIRED ITS BEAUTY, WISHING IT WAS HIS. THE MORE HE THOUGHT ABOUT IT THE MORE HE WANTED HIS NEIGHBOR'S PROPERTY. THE COMMANDMENT SAYS, "THOU SHALT NOT COVET," BUT AHAB DID NOT REGARD JEHOVAH.

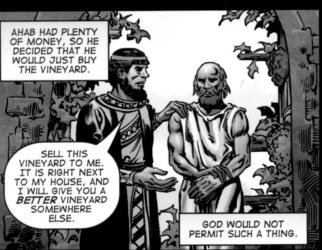

AHAB HAD PLENTY OF MONEY, SO HE DECIDED THAT HE WOULD JUST BUY THE VINEYARD.

SELL THIS VINEYARD TO ME. IT IS RIGHT NEXT TO MY HOUSE, AND I WILL GIVE YOU A *BETTER* VINEYARD SOMEWHERE ELSE.

GOD WOULD NOT PERMIT SUCH A THING.

THIS PROPERTY HAS BEEN IN MY FAMILY FOR OVER *500* YEARS. THE LAW COMMANDS US NOT TO SELL OUR LAND OUTSIDE THE FAMILY.

TELL ME, MY DEAR, WHY DO YOU NOT *EAT?* WHY ARE YOU SO *SAD?*

BECAUSE *NABOTH* WILL NOT SELL HIS VINEYARD TO ME.

YOU ARE THE KING. YOU HAVE THE POWER TO DO *ANYTHING YOU PLEASE.* DON'T LET ONE LOWLY PEASANT STAND IN THE WAY OF YOUR *HAPPINESS.* I WILL GET THE VINEYARD FOR YOU.

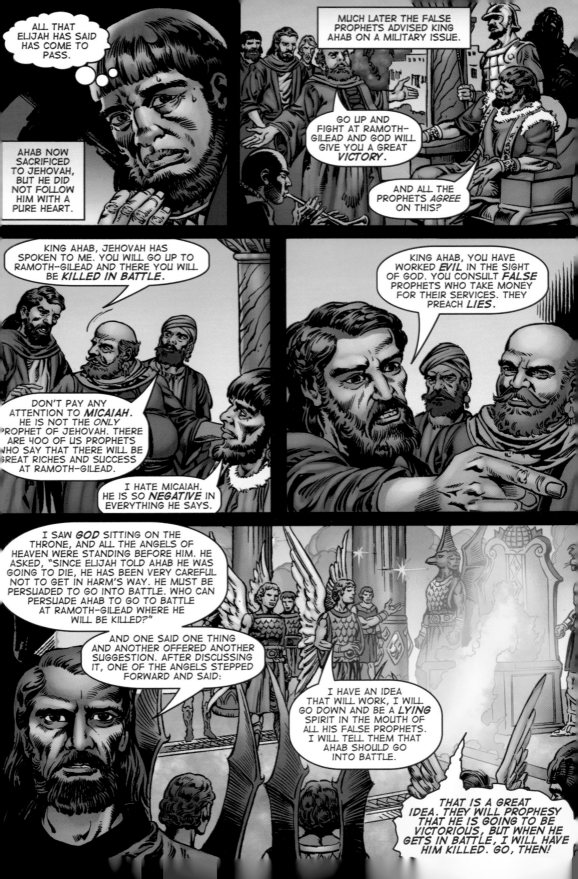

A SOLDIER SHOT AN ARROW HIGH IN THE AIR, NOT AIMING AT ANYONE IN PARTICULAR, JUST HOPING TO HIT ONE OF HIS ENEMIES.

THUD!

UGGGHH!

WHAT?

HURRY, IT IS BLEEDING BADLY.

HANG ON!

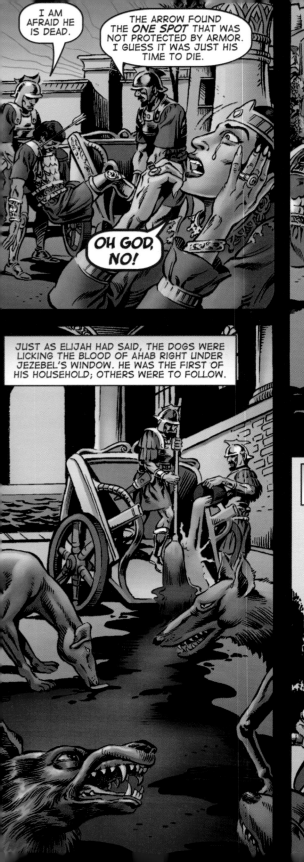

YOU FOOL! YOU ARE NOT A PROPHET OF GOD. YOU ARE A LIAR! AHAB IS DEAD JUST AS MICAIAH THE PROPHET OF JEHOVAH DECLARED.

YOU ARE FREE TO GO. AHAB IS DEAD.

BUT IT CAN'T BE. ALL THE DEVOUT MEN AGREED. AHAB WOULD BE VICTORIOUS.

NOT ALL. NOT MICAIAH WHOM YOU SLAPPED AND PUT IN PRISON. WHEN THE PEOPLE HEAR OF THIS THEY WILL HAVE YOUR HEAD.

YES I KNOW, AND NO DOUBT THE DOGS HAVE LICKED HIS BLOOD AS GOD SAID. JEZEBEL WILL BE NEXT AND ALL THAT ARE RELATED TO AHAB. GOD HAS SPOKEN.

OH NO! MICAIAH SAID I WOULD KNOW WHO HAD THE SPIRIT OF GOD ON THE DAY I HID IN A SMALL ROOM INSIDE OF A ROOM.

I MUST HIDE.

AHAB'S SONS WOULD REIGN IN HIS PLACE, AND TWELVE YEARS WOULD PASS WITH JEZEBEL STILL LIVING AS QUEEN. ISRAEL WOULD CONTINUE TO WORSHIP FALSE GODS AND BREAK THE COMMANDMENTS OF GOD.

GOD SPOKE AGAINST THE HOUSE OF AHAB, SAYING, "THE TIME HAS COME. ALL OF AHAB'S FAMILY WILL PERISH, EVEN THE LITTLE CHILDREN. NONE WILL BE LEFT ALIVE. JEZEBEL WILL BE EATEN BY THE DOGS, AND THERE WILL BE NO ONE TO MOURN HER OR BURY HER."

12 YEARS LATER.

I MUST PAINT MY FACE, SO I WILL BE ATTRACTIVE TO GENERAL JEHU WHEN HE RETURNS FROM BATTLE.

WROARRRR

THE CHARIOT OF FIRE SEPARATED ELIJAH FROM ELISHA.

ELIJAH WAS TAKEN UP TO HEAVEN IN THE WHIRLWIND.

THEN ALL WAS QUIET. ELIJAH WAS NOW IN GOD'S PRESENCE.

ALL THAT IS LEFT IS HIS MANTLE. IT IS WHAT HE USED TO PART THE WATERS.

2 KINGS 2:11-13

KINGSTONE COMICS

KINGSTONECOMICS.COM